Exploring
Villages

Katie Orchard

HODDER
Wayland

an imprint of Hodder Children's Books

Titles in this series:
Seaside Towns
Villages

Exploring Villages is a simplified and updated version of Hodder Wayland's *Landmarks: Exploring Villages*

Text copyright © Hodder Wayland 2004
Volume copyright © Hodder Wayland 2004

Editor: Katie Sergeant
Designers: Tim Mayer/Mark Whitchurch
Typesetter: Jane Hawkins
Cover design: Hodder Children's Books

First published in 1997 by Wayland Publishers Ltd.
This edition updated and published in 2004 by
Hodder Wayland, an imprint of Hodder Children's Books

Orchard, Katie
    Exploring Villages
    1. Villages – Great Britain – Juvenile literature 2. Country
    life – Great Britain – Juvenile literature 3. Villages –
    Great Britain – History – Juvenile literature 4. Country
    life – Great Britain – History – Juvenile literature
    I. Title
    307.7'62'0941

ISBN 075024609X

Printed in China

Hodder Children's Books
A division of Hodder Headline Limited
338 Euston Road, London NW1 3BH

Cover: Cottages on a hill in Shaftesbury; **inset picture:** Farmer worming sheep.
Title page: Bodinnick fishing village, in Cornwall.
Contents page: A children's farm.

Picture acknowledgements:
Cover (inset) Agripicture Images/Alamy Peter Dean, **(main)** Photodisc Green/Getty Jeremy Woodhouse **CEPHAS** Frank B. Higham 11 (left), 26 (bottom); **James Davis Travel Photography** 5 (top); **East Sussex County Council** 7 (bottom right), 43; **Eye Ubiquitous** 5 Simon Warner (bottom), P. Craven 21; **Goodness Gracious** 25 Keith Harding; **Hodder Wayland Picture Library** 16; **Impact Photos** John Arthur 34 and 40 (bottom), Alan Blair 8, Julian Calder 40, Piers Cavendish 15, Christopher Cormack 28, Robert Eames 6, David Gallant 10, Tony Page 19 (bottom), Caroline Penn 37 (bottom), Simon Shepheard 9 (bottom), 14, 27 (bottom), 33 (top), 38, 39, Bruce Stephens 4, 9 (top), 32, 33 (bottom), John Walmsley title page, Stewart Weir contents page, 11 (right), 12, 13 (top), 17 (both), 18, 19 (top right), 20, 23, 24, 26 (top), 30, 31, 37 (top), 41; **Ordnance Survey** 7 (top left); **Rural Development Commission** 13 (bottom), 22 (both), 35 (both), 42; **Simon Warner** 5 (bottom).

Every effort has been made to contact the people featured in the case studies of the original version of this book, and to check the facts and figures. If any factual details are now incorrect, the Publisher will make the necessary changes in any further reprintings of this title.

Contents

Words in **bold** can be found in the glossary.

What is a Village?

A village is a small **settlement** often in a **rural** area. Villages can be found on the coast as well as inland. They have much smaller populations than towns or cities. Village populations are more spread out than those in cities.

Some villages have only a few houses, clustered around a farm. Others are larger, with a high street, shops, a church, a school and a village hall. Many villages have very old buildings. In some growing villages, modern buildings and new housing estates stand alongside fifteenth-century houses.

In Meriden, Warwickshire, modern, red-brick houses have been built beside traditional thatched cottages. ▼

RURAL POPULATIONS

Hamlet	10–100
Small village	100–500
Large village	500–2,000

4

Rolling hills surround the village of Gunnerside, in North Yorkshire. ▶

During the **Industrial Revolution** of the early 1800s, many villagers moved to the bustling cities in search of work. Today, rail and road networks allow more people to live in villages and work in towns and cities.

Uig, on the Isle of Skye, is made up of just a few scattered houses. ▼

Different types of village

There are different types of villages. Some villages have grown up around a village green or pond. Other villages developed in a line along the length of a road. All the important buildings, such as the school and church, are found in the centre. In **remote** areas, houses with large plots of land are scattered over the hillsides.

Many village **settlements** were built around important natural features. Springs and rivers attracted settlers because they provided clean drinking water. Some villages developed around areas of fertile land, which was good for farming. Other villages grew up around artificial features, such as crossroads, bridges or wells.

◀ Blaenau Ffestiniog, in North Wales, grew up around a slate quarry.

◀ This map shows the village of East Hoathly, in East Sussex.

▲ This **aerial photograph** shows the same area as the map.

ACTIVITY

The map above has symbols for a church ✝, school (Sch) and post office (PO).

Find these landmarks on the aerial photograph (above right).

During the **Industrial Revolution** some factory owners built '**model villages**' to house their workers. Bournville, near Birmingham, was built by George Cadbury, the chocolate maker.

Large factories required huge amounts of coal to fuel their machinery. Much of Britain's coal was mined in **rural** areas, such as the Welsh valleys, Yorkshire and Ayrshire, in Scotland. Villages grew up around the **collieries**. Today, many collieries have closed down, but the villages are still there.

Village Life

Some people have lived in villages for their whole lives. Their families may have lived in the same area for generations. Many people living in small villages will know everyone else that lives there. In larger villages people do not always know each other, but the whole community may share the same doctor, school and shops.

Only about 10 per cent of people in the UK live in villages. This is set to change as more people are choosing to move to the countryside.

▲ Linton-in-Craven, in Yorkshire, has a village green where people can get together and children can play.

Who lives in a village?

Before the **Industrial Revolution**, most people in the UK lived and worked in villages. Soon, new factories sprang up in towns all around the UK. Huge numbers of villagers moved to the growing towns in search of work.

Today, the number of people moving to villages is rising. Many people now prefer to live in leafy villages and **commute** to work in cities and towns nearby. Some elderly people also move to villages when they retire. With so many people moving to villages, house prices in these areas have risen. Many young villagers now cannot afford to buy their own homes.

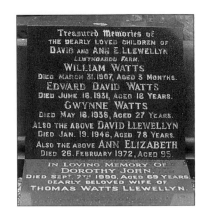

▲ Gravestones show how long families have lived in the same village.

◄ Village squares provide a place for the whole community to get together. These children are dancing round a maypole.

9

Houses and homes

Most of the oldest village houses were made from local materials. Limestone was a popular building material in the Cotswolds. In Cumbria, homes were usually built from whitewashed stone. In Devon, many old houses still have roofs made from thatch.

Many village homes today were once farm buildings. Some Sussex barns and Kent **oast houses** have been converted into modern homes with central heating and double glazing.

Skilled craftspeople cut and shape layers of reeds to make a thatched roof. ▼

Many villages are growing as people move there from towns and cities. New housing estates are often built on disused farmland at the edge of the original village. Sometimes these estates are named after the features that were there before they were built, such as Meadow Way or Orchard Lane.

▲ This modern housing estate has been built on the site of an old mill.

◄ Oast houses were traditionally used to store hops for making beer. This one is now a home.

Getting together

Village communities may be small or **isolated**. It is important for villagers to be able to meet their neighbours and talk about what is happening in the area.

Local churches often hold events on their grounds, such as summer fêtes or local festivals. Village halls are used for all kinds of activities, from local competitions to fundraising events, such as jumble sales, to raise money for local projects.

Village fêtes provide the community with a chance to get together. ▼

▲ A family enjoys a meal in a village pub garden.

Pubs are an important part of village life. They provide a relaxed and friendly place for villagers to meet each other. Many village pubs have gardens outside, where the whole family is welcome.

Kentisbeare Village Hall, Devon

It took six years of hard work for villagers in Kentisbeare to raise enough money to build their village hall. Fundraising activities included a summer fête with a hot-air balloon, bingo nights and 'safari suppers', where people travelled from one house to another to eat a different course. The hall was finally built in 1994.

The whole community now uses the hall. Children from the local school even have their PE lessons there. The hall is also the setting for a youth club and a playgroup.

Kentisbeare Village Hall, in Devon, gives villagers a place to play sports, such as badminton. ▶

Traditions and change

Modern village life is very different from how it used to be. Traditional industries, such as farming, fishing or mining, have now **declined**. Today, many villagers **commute** to work in cities and towns. Others may only have work in the village for part of the year, such as during the tourist season.

Many villagers now travel to larger towns for shopping or entertainment. As a result in some areas local shops and village halls have had to close down.

In Hope, in Derbyshire, the old tradition of well-dressing (see page 15) continues today. ▼

Although village life is changing, many traditions still remain. In some Peak District villages, wells are blessed and decorated with flower pictures to give thanks for fresh water. In the **pit villages** of Nottinghamshire and Yorkshire, Miners' Galas are still held each year to celebrate the traditional mining industry.

◀ Agricultural shows are traditional village events, where farmers display their best animals and local people have a chance to meet up.

Work

In the UK today only a small number of villagers work on the land. Many villagers **commute** to the nearest town or city to work in a variety of places, including shops, offices, banks and schools.

About 75 per cent of land in the UK is farmed, but only about half a million people in the UK work in the farming industry.

In the past, most villagers worked by hand on farmland nearby. During the **Agricultural Revolution**, fast, new farm machinery replaced the need for farm workers. Wealthy landowners took over common land, so ordinary people could no longer grow food on it.

◄ This combine harvester can do the work of many people, and in less time.

Finished trugs (traditional wooden baskets) for sale. ▼

Robin Tuppen, Trug-maker

Trugs are traditional wooden Sussex baskets. Robin Tuppen has been making trugs for 14 years. He runs his own workshop near Chidingleigh, in East Sussex, selling trugs, made in the traditional way. Robin employs 12 skilled craftspeople.

Robin says, "*Today, trugs are only made in a few places. We sell our trugs all over the world.*"

Reg Saunders made trugs for 34 years. He has now retired. ▼

Before the **Industrial Revolution**, whole families worked in **cottage industries**, making goods by hand, such as furniture or clothes. Other villagers may have worked in large, country houses as servants or gardeners. In small **pit villages** most people were miners.

17

Farming and fishing

Jonathan Tate, Lime Cross Nursery

Jonathan Tate has lived in Herstmonceux, in East Sussex, all his life. He runs a successful nursery called Lime Cross. The land has been in Jonathan's family for over 50 years, but it wasn't always a nursery.

Jonathan explains, "*My parents first used the land as a pig farm and for market gardening. I now grow conifer trees and other plants that are sold to garden centres across the country.*"

Modern farming methods such as **factory farming** have led to fewer jobs. The European Union (EU) has made changes to the way land is farmed by 'setting aside' land. This means that some fields must be left empty so that farmers do not grow too much of a particular crop. Fewer farm workers are needed to work the land. Market gardening (growing fruit and vegetables) still employs many people, but only during harvest time.

Fishing is still important in some coastal villages. However, larger fishing boats from other countries can catch more fish and sell them at lower prices. This has made it difficult for smaller fishing businesses to survive.

◄ Jonathan Tate's nursery employs five full-time gardeners.

Tourism

Tourism also provides jobs for villagers, but often only during the summer. Most villagers employed in the tourist industry work in cafés, hotels and restaurants.

▲ **Rural** farm centres are popular village tourist attractions that provide work for some local people.

◄ The fishing industry still employs many people in some coastal villages.

New jobs for villagers

Unemployment is rising in villages. **Planners** are trying to create new jobs for local people by encouraging new businesses to set up in **rural** areas. Old, disused farm buildings are now being turned into offices and workshops.

Villages are not as **isolated** as they used to be. With improvements in road and rail networks, and new technology, many businesses no longer need to be based in towns or cities. Some new businesses are now choosing to move to rural areas, where office space is often cheaper than in the cities. Rural business parks, where several small factory units are based in the same area, are becoming popular.

This rural business park on the outskirts of Uckfield has brought many jobs back to the area. ▼

▲ In the Peak District, dry stone walls are still used to divide up the land.

Traditional skills

In some rural areas, traditional village crafts are still practised so that they will not die out. Skilled craftspeople are teaching young **apprentices** the art of dry stone walling (building walls without cement), and thatching. In villages where horse-riding is popular, saddle-making and the blacksmith's craft (making horse shoes) are thriving.

ACTIVITY

A visitors' centre may tell you about traditional local products or skills and how employment in the area has changed. There may be one near where you live. Collect souvenirs of your visit and make a scrapbook.

In some villages, visitors' centres have been set up to show people how work in the area may have changed.

The Wensleydale Creamery, near Hawes in Yorkshire, opened its visitors' centre after the cheese-making factory closed down. Visitors find out how cheese is made and the centre also provides some jobs in the area.

◄ The Wensleydale Creamery visitors' centre shows people how cheese is made. It also has a cheese shop and a coffee shop. ▼

With the help of money from the government, many villages have set up 'telecottage centres'. These centres give local people a chance to learn computer skills. In some coal-mining communities, where the **collieries** have closed down, ex-miners are using their new computer skills to run their own businesses.

Retained fire-fighters can be called to an emergency at any time. ▼

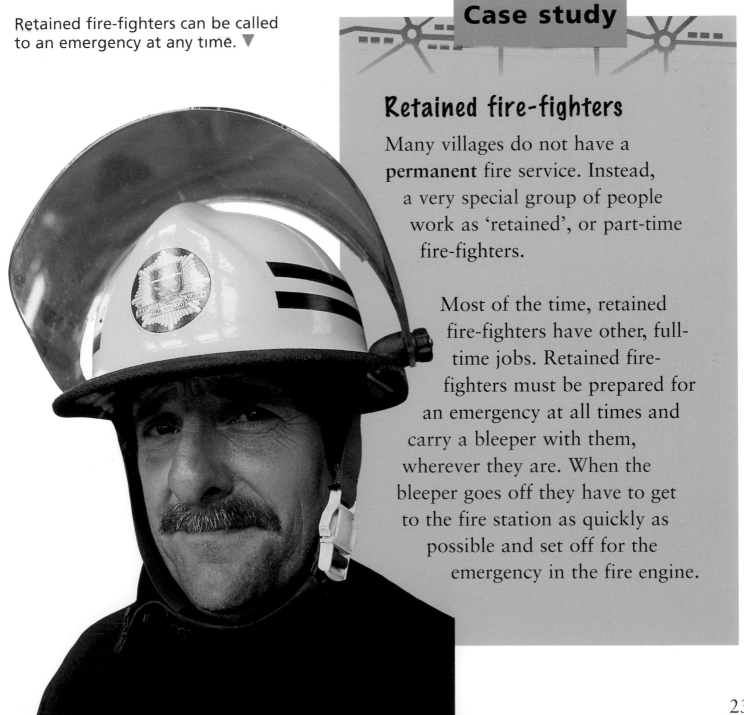

Case study

Retained fire-fighters

Many villages do not have a **permanent** fire service. Instead, a very special group of people work as 'retained', or part-time fire-fighters.

Most of the time, retained fire-fighters have other, full-time jobs. Retained fire-fighters must be prepared for an emergency at all times and carry a bleeper with them, wherever they are. When the bleeper goes off they have to get to the fire station as quickly as possible and set off for the emergency in the fire engine.

Village Schools

Most village schools serve a small area, usually just the village itself. In **remote** areas, where the population is more spread out, one school may have pupils from several different villages.

Village schools are usually smaller than those found in cities or towns. It is not unusual for a village school to have fewer than 50 pupils. This is very different from an inner-city primary school, which may have more than 500 pupils.

Many village schools have large playing fields and wide, open spaces. ▼

▲ Oakwood School, in Surrey, had to close in 1994 when the number of pupils fell too low. This photograph was taken on the last day.

Village schools also have much smaller class sizes than those in **urban** areas. Some primary schools may have only one classroom, shared by children from the ages of 5 to 11.

If the number of pupils in a small school falls, it may become too expensive to run and the school may be forced to close down. The remaining pupils may then have to travel further to reach to the nearest school.

School buildings

Some village schools are very old. They may have been built more than 200 years ago by a wealthy landowner, or by the local church. Generations of the same family may have gone to the same school. Other schools are much more modern, built by the council to cope with newcomers that have moved to new housing developments in the village.

◀ A modern village school.

With smaller class sizes, it is easier for village schools to have lessons outside on a sunny day. ▶

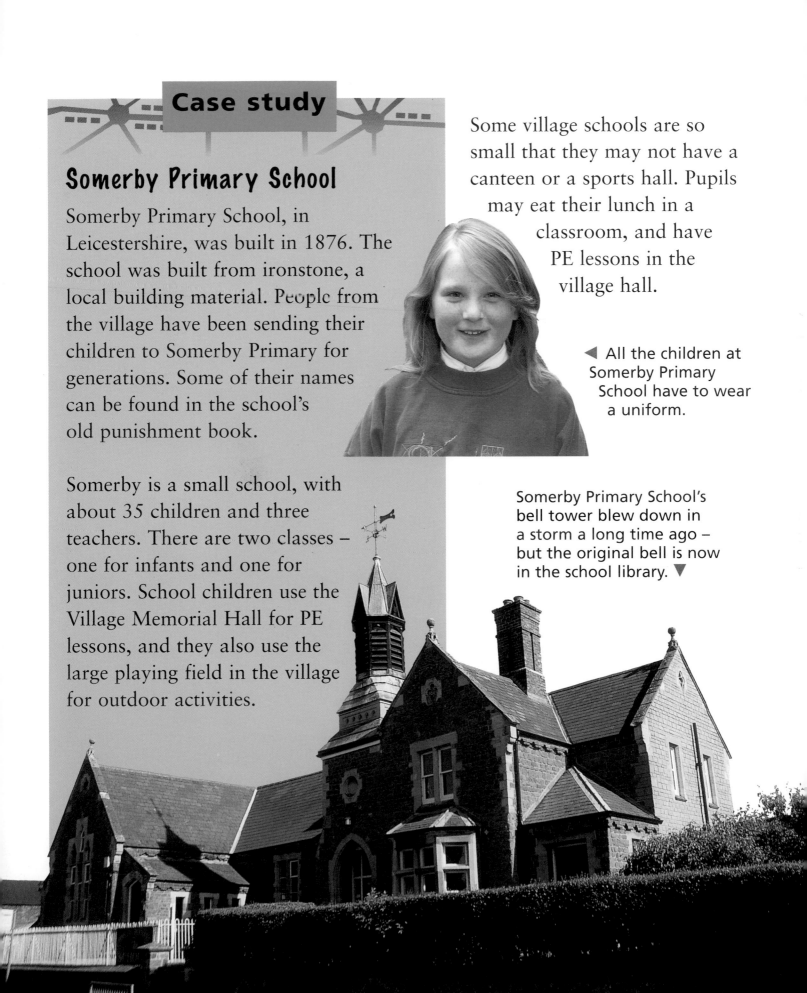

Somerby Primary School

Somerby Primary School, in Leicestershire, was built in 1876. The school was built from ironstone, a local building material. People from the village have been sending their children to Somerby Primary for generations. Some of their names can be found in the school's old punishment book.

Somerby is a small school, with about 35 children and three teachers. There are two classes – one for infants and one for juniors. School children use the Village Memorial Hall for PE lessons, and they also use the large playing field in the village for outdoor activities.

Some village schools are so small that they may not have a canteen or a sports hall. Pupils may eat their lunch in a classroom, and have PE lessons in the village hall.

◄ All the children at Somerby Primary School have to wear a uniform.

Somerby Primary School's bell tower blew down in a storm a long time ago – but the original bell is now in the school library. ▼

Green spaces

One of the big advantages of a village school is that there are lots of wide open spaces nearby. Nature trails and local beauty spots are much easier to visit in the countryside than they would be for schools in **urban** areas.

◀ For some children living in the Scottish islands, the nearest school is a boat ride away.

School journeys

Some village children may have to travel a long way to get to school. **Rural** areas have few bus services, so parents often take their children to school by car. In very **remote** areas, the school journey can be quite difficult. Children living on some Scottish islands have to take a boat to get to school.

ACTIVITY

Draw a simple plan of your school.

You will need: a tape measure, a ruler, graph paper, a pencil and some coloured pencils.

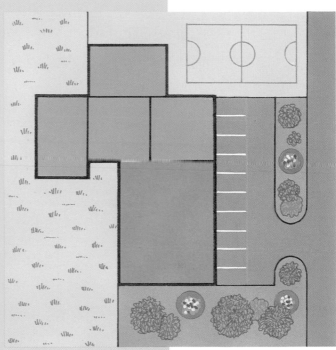

1. Using the tape measure, measure the outer walls of the school building and the edge of the school grounds. Choose a scale that fits on your graph paper.
Try 1 metre = 1 square.

2. Draw the school building and grounds on your graph paper with a pencil and ruler.

3. Measure the playground, playing field and car park. Draw these areas on to your plan.

4. Add other features to your plan, such as classrooms, flower beds and goal posts. Make a note of the distance between one object and another.

5. Colour in your finished plan, and remember to add a key.

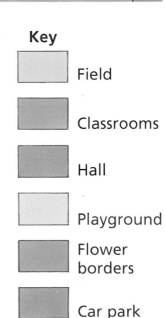

Key

Field

Classrooms

Hall

Playground

Flower borders

Car park

Transport

Villages are often more difficult to reach than **urban** areas. It is important for villagers to be able to travel around easily, so that they do not feel cut off.

In 1973 there were 13.5 million cars on UK roads.

By 2003 the figure had risen to over 24 million.

People living in villages may have to travel long distances to go shopping or to use other important services such as hospitals or schools.

▲ This peaceful cycle track used to be a busy railway line.

◀ Village train platforms are often busy with commuters during rush hours.

The rail network

Until about 200 years ago, many villages were cut off from the rest of the country. This began to change during the 'Railway Age' of the 1800s, when thousands of kilometres of railways were built, gradually linking towns and villages all over the UK.

By the 1930s many **rural** areas were connected to the rail network. Many people moved to new housing estates in villages on the outskirts of cities, where they could **commute** to work by train. As some cities grew, these villages were swallowed up to become **suburbs** of the cities.

Buses

Many villages have only a few bus services, while others have no bus service at all. In villages with a small population, bus companies cannot afford to run a service for so few customers.

▲ The village bus in Creigiau, in Wales, takes villagers to Cardiff and back.

Cars

Today most villagers rely on cars to get around. However, fast-moving cars on **rural** roads are dangerous to pedestrians. Some villages have traffic calming systems, which are coloured road surfaces (see photograph on page 33), to remind drivers to slow down.

ACTIVITY

In Belfast, in Northern Ireland, most facilities are within 2 kilometres of the centre. But for villagers living in Carnlough, the nearest hospital is in Antrim, 48 kilometres away!

Pick a village and a town near you. Using an Ordnance Survey map of the village and a town plan, compare how far people living in each place have to travel to get to the nearest hospital, supermarket and leisure centre. Record your findings in a table.

▲ The post bus service is particularly popular with the elderly.

Case study

Post buses

Post buses have been introduced in **remote** areas, such as parts of Staffordshire, where there is little or no public transport. As well as collecting and delivering mail, post buses provide transport for local people. Some post buses even have wheelchair ramps.

More cars in a village means more pollution. Local wildlife and buildings can also be damaged by traffic fumes. Quiet roads soon become jammed with extra traffic. Village roads simply cannot cope with the rising number of cars.

Yet, many villagers depend on cars to help them get around. Shops and services may be several kilometres away from a village. With few buses or trains, villagers without cars feel very **isolated**.

Traffic calming reminds drivers to slow down when driving through a village. ▼

33

Shops and Entertainment

Unlike cities and towns, many villages do not have supermarkets, theatres, cinemas, banks or leisure centres.

If a village does have its own shop, it usually provides the local community with many different services, all under one roof. As well as selling groceries, village shops are often places where local people meet to share news, buy stamps and even hire videos or DVDs. Some village shops also sell local crafts and goods.

Rural Development Commission survey of 8,000 UK villages:

No post office: 43 per cent

No **permanent** shop: 40 per cent

No village hall: 29 per cent

No bank: 90 per cent

This is the main shopping street in Burford, in Oxfordshire. ▼

Village shops often face competition from out-of-town superstores. Many village shops now provide other services, such as delivering groceries to their customers' homes, and Internet access, to encourage villagers to shop there.

Long Preston Post Office, North Yorkshire

The post office at Long Preston sells a lot more than stamps. Local people visit the shop to buy groceries, newspapers and wine. The shop also provides photocopying, faxing, photo developing and word-processing services. And with no chemist in the village, people even pop into the post office to pick up prescriptions from the local doctor.

▲ The post office shelves are packed with more than 3,000 different types of groceries.

▲ Long Preston Post Office provides a valuable service to the community.

Travelling services

In villages that do not have a **permanent** shop, a **mobile** shop may visit the area once or twice a week. Mobile libraries also provide a useful service, giving villagers a chance to borrow books or videos, once a week.

Meeting people

The village hall and pub are popular places for villagers to get together and catch up on local news. The local church is often the centre for local events, such as village fêtes. Many outdoor activities may take place on the village green or recreation ground.

ACTIVITY

Make a survey of what your friends and family like to do in their spare time. Draw up a table like the one below and give each activity a separate column. Note the number of people that you surveyed.

Activity	Number of people
Cinema	4
Swimming	6
Restaurant	2
Reading	3
Football/cricket	5
Country walks	4

Present your information in a bar chart like the one on the right. Which activity is the most popular?

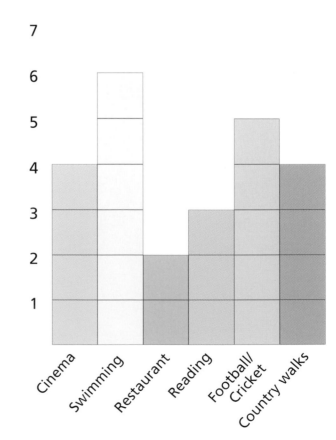

Getting out and about

Many young people feel that there is not enough for them to do in a village. Facilities such as leisure centres or cinemas are often several kilometres away.

Some villages have set up special outdoor centres so that young local people can learn new activities, such as abseiling or climbing.

Walking, rambling and cycling are all popular activities in **rural** areas. A network of cycle paths and footpaths criss-cross large areas of countryside. Golf centres, riding stables and visitors' centres also encourage people to get out and about in rural areas.

▲ Some villages have their own adventure playground for children to explore.

Many people enjoy walking in the peaceful beauty of the countryside. ▼

Villages and Change

Like any other type of **settlement**, villages are constantly changing. Many villagers enjoy the calm and green environment of village life. For others, especially older people and young families with no transport of their own, village life may feel quite lonely.

Changes in a village may also affect local wildlife. In some Yorkshire coal-mining areas, a type of moth turned black, allowing it to hide among plants that were blackened with coal dust. When the coal industry declined, the moth's wings began to return to their original white colour.

Beautiful scenery and a peaceful environment attract many newcomers to **rural** areas and village needs may change to cope with the rising population. Transport, schools, housing, and jobs are all important village issues.

Increasing numbers of cars on the roads mean that traffic jams are becoming common in some villages. ▶

Pleaseley Vale Business Park, Derbyshire

In some areas, disused buildings have been given a new lease of life. In Pleaseley Vale, an old Victorian textile mill was converted to make workspaces and offices. The business park is set in a conservation area, surrounded by beautiful countryside. There are three large stone buildings for factory use, and two smaller lodges containing office spaces.

The business park has been a valuable addition to the area, encouraging businesses to move there.

Planners need to make sure that they look at all the needs of villagers, and make useful improvements without losing the charm and character of the area. New housing and schools may be built, and many planners are trying to attract new businesses to rural areas to create more jobs.

Pleaseley Vale Business Park was once a vandalised, derelict building. ▼

While it is important to create new jobs in **rural** areas, **planners** need to make sure that new projects do not damage the fragile environment.

As well as trying to attract new businesses to villages, villagers themselves must continue to spend money in the area. Villagers and tourists are encouraged to buy locally produced food and goods. This allows local businesses to continue to thrive. Some villagers may even buy shares in a local shop to keep it going.

▲ Peat-cutting in Scotland. Peat is used in the whisky industry, but harvesting it can damage the land.

Tourists spend money in tea shops and country pubs. ▶

Many **parish councils** are now listening to younger people's opinions. If villagers of all ages feel that their views and needs are important, the more likely they are not to move away. Many village communities are working hard to improve village life.

Some villages have their own youth clubs, where teenagers can get together after school. ▼

ACTIVITY

Perhaps you would like to improve your school environment. Carry out a survey among your friends to find out which changes they would most like to see.

Here are some examples of questions you might ask:

- Is there enough space to play sports, such as football?
- Would you like to have a special nature area, with wild flowers to attract insects?
- Do you want to have more after-school clubs?

Display your findings in a table or present your results using computer graphics.

Finding Out More

There are many ways to find out more about a village.

See for yourself
The village post office or shop may have a notice board with information about local events, jobs and services on offer. Local newspapers may include news about daily life and people's views in the area.

Ask around
People you know, such as family members, teachers or neighbours, may have lived in a village. Ask them about daily life there.

Your local library may have all kinds of information about villages. The librarian will be able to help you find maps, reference books, magazines and newspapers.

The local **parish council** can send you information about future plans for the area. The County Record Office will have old maps and parish records that give you interesting details about the village's past.

The Internet
If you have access to a computer, the Internet can provide all kinds of information about a particular village, including the shops, hotels and other businesses in the area.

Maps

Several different types of map will give you information about an area. A road atlas will show where a village is in the UK. Village street plans give a little more information and can sometimes be found in a map book covering the whole county. For even more detail, find an Ordnance Survey map of the village.

Census information

Census information gives details about how many people live in an area, how old they are, what jobs they do, what type of home they live in and whether or not they own a car. You can find census information in a large public library, or on the Internet.

Tourist information

Tourist information centres can tell you about museums, **rural** visitor's centres and other places to visit in the local area.

Village scrapbook

Once you have collected all your information, you can make a scrapbook of your chosen village. Include leaflets, postcards, tourist information, maps and tape recordings of interviews.

Notes For Adults

This book is designed to be an introduction to villages and their communities. The book looks at various aspects of village life, including village homes, jobs, schools and communities. Several types of village are explored and this book can be used by children who live in any type of settlement as a comparative guide.

Case studies in each chapter provide specific information about a particular aspect of village life. Some provide direct quotes from villagers to give first-hand information. Children can use this information to make a direct comparison with their own experiences.

This book also includes several simple activities. They have been designed so that children from any type of settlement can attempt them. Some of the activities may demonstrate a particular point that has been made about villages. Others may be used to demonstrate a contrast between villages and other types of settlement. Children are encouraged to use some of the methods employed by geographers to find evidence or present data, such as mapping and graph skills, conducting surveys and using primary source material such as interviews or census data.

What is a Village? (pages 4–7)

This chapter gives a brief overview of different types of village found in the UK. The language and examples used encourage children to look around them and either compare or contrast their own settlement with that of a particular village. The text examines why some villages are situated in specific locations and how they differ from one another.

Activity on page 7:
This activity is designed to illustrate how an aerial photograph compares with an Ordnance Survey map of the same area. Children are invited to identify objects and features shown on the map using a simple key, and then to see whether they can find the same features on the aerial photograph.

Village Life (pages 8–15)

This chapter looks at the 'sense of community' in a small settlement. Children are encouraged to think about what this means, by looking at who might live in a village and what their needs might be. Village buildings and focal points of village life are also explored. How does village life compare with the child's own experiences?

Work (pages 16–23)

This chapter deals with the village economy, including traditional types of employment and how this has changed today. Children are encouraged to think about land use, and how the nature of a particular settlement is reflected in the type of employment available in the area. Ask the child to think of the types of employment that are found in their own settlement, and to compare and contrast them with those mentioned in the text.

Activity on page 22:
This activity encourages children to think about the history of their local area, by going to a visitors' centre and collecting evidence for themselves. It also invites them to develop presentation skills.

Village Schools (pages 24–29)

This chapter allows children to compare or contrast their own school with those in the text. How many children attend their school? Is their class small or large? Are there children of different ages in the same class?

Activity on page 29:

This simple mapping activity involves thinking about size, proportion and the purpose of using a key on maps to differentiate between different types of land use.

Transport (pages 30–33)

In this chapter children are encouraged to think about the importance of good communication and transport links to a particular community. They should think about how they get to school, the effect of more cars on the road, and the benefits of public transport.

Activity on page 32:

This activity shows the distances villagers may have to travel to get to certain facilities, compared with a town. They may be encouraged to think about which services are most important to them, and whether having to travel long distances to go to the cinema, for example, might affect where they choose to live. Children can produce a table to compare their two chosen localities.

Shops and Entertainment (pages 34–37)

This chapter shows how the character of a village is reflected in the local shops and facilities, and how these are changing to meet the needs of the villagers.

Activity on page 36:

This activity invites children to take account of differing opinions by conducting a survey. They are then encouraged to think about how to present their results visually, in a bar chart.

Villages and Change (pages 38–41)

This chapter demonstrates that while rural areas are attractive places to live, they may also seem isolating to some people. It also looks at how planners need to consider the opinions of the whole community before making any changes to the area.

Activity on page 41:

This survey encourages children to consider the opinions of their peers, and also to think about change and how this might affect them. If they have access to a computer, they could present their findings using computer graphics.

Finding Out More (pages 42-43)

This section may provide some useful ideas on how to start researching a particular village. It is only intended as a starting point, not as a definitive guide.

Glossary

aerial photograph A photograph of an area, taken from a high place, such as an aeroplane.

Agricultural Revolution A period during the eighteenth century, when new farm machinery was developed. The new machines took the place of many farm workers, who had done the same work by hand.

apprentices People who learn a traditional trade or craft from a skilled craftsperson.

census A survey of the population. It is carried out every ten years.

collieries Coal mines and their workings.

commute To travel a long way to get to work.

cottage industries Industries based on work that was done by hand, often by several members of the same family.

declined Fallen in number.

factory farming Modern farming methods that mean many animals are kept in the same place and much of the work is done by machines.

Industrial Revolution A period during the eighteenth and nineteenth centuries, when new machinery led to the growth of factories.

isolated Far away from any other type of settlement or facilities.

mobile Moving from one place to another.

model villages Villages built by factory owners to house their workers during the Industrial Revolution.

oast houses Farm buildings that were once used to store hops, which are used in the beer-making process.

parish council A group of people that have been chosen to manage several village communities in a rural area.

permanent Something that is always there.

pit villages Villages that grew up around the coal mining industry.

planners People that make plans about the future development of an area.

remote Far away from anywhere else.

rural In the countryside.

settlement An area where people live.

suburbs Areas of housing on the outskirts of a city.

urban Built-up areas with high populations.

Books To Read

Changing Face of the UK by Rob Bowden (Hodder Wayland, 2004)

United Kingdom (Countries of the World) by Rob Bowden (Evans, 2002)

Farming (Earth in Danger) by Polly Goodman (Hodder Wayland, 2001)

Food and Farming (Geography for Fun) by Pam Robson (Watts, 2003)

Settlements (Earth in Danger) by Polly Goodman (Hodder Wayland, 2001)

This map shows the villages mentioned in the book.

Index